Images and Pictures You Should Not Masturbate To

The Ultimate Picture Book of Images You Can Pleasure Yourself To... But Probably Shouldn't!

Jakov Cumming

ISBN-13: **978-1539090496**

WARNING

Throughout history people have warned against the dangers of masturbation, fapping, playing the skin flute, wanking, choking the chicken, playing with yourself, flicking the bean, firing off some knuckle children, going to the palm prom, jerking the gerkin, jacking off and whatever euphemistic phrase you wish to employ.

Masturbation is known to cause the following terrible side effects:-

- Blindness
- Lose of strength and athletic prowess
- An eternity of damnation in the fires of Hell
- Loss of appetite
- Sleepiness
- Friction burn

As the above list of dangers suggests, masturbation is no laughing matter. It is in no way funny, humorous, satirical, fun or pleasurable. MASTURBATION IS A SERIOUS ISSUE WITH SERIOUS DANGERS.

This book has been designed by Jakov Cummings for the sole purpose of inspiring all who see it to never masturbate again!

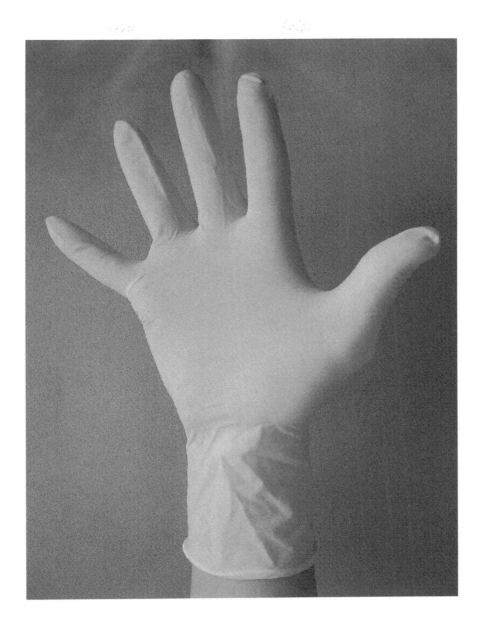

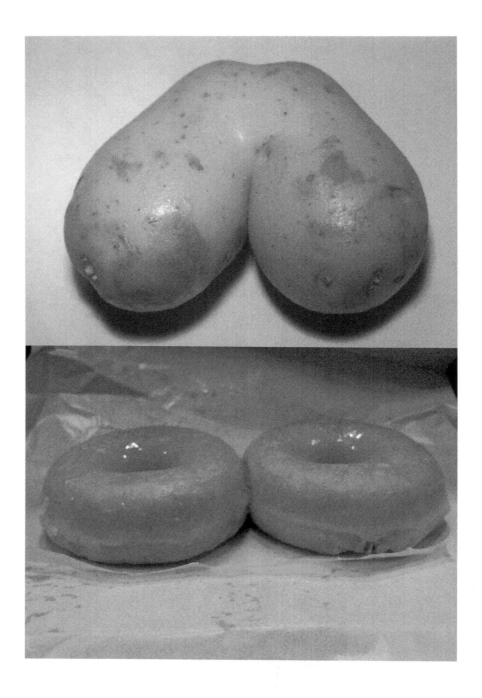

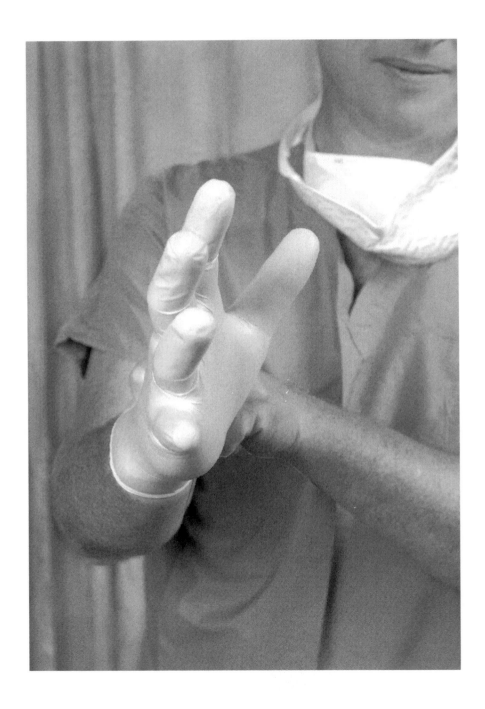

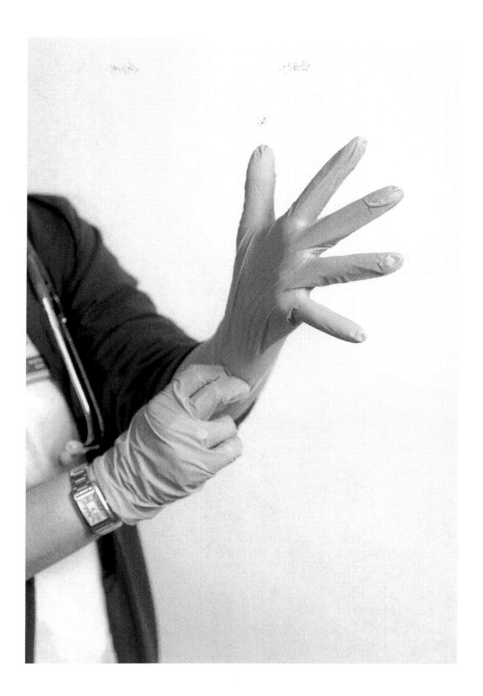

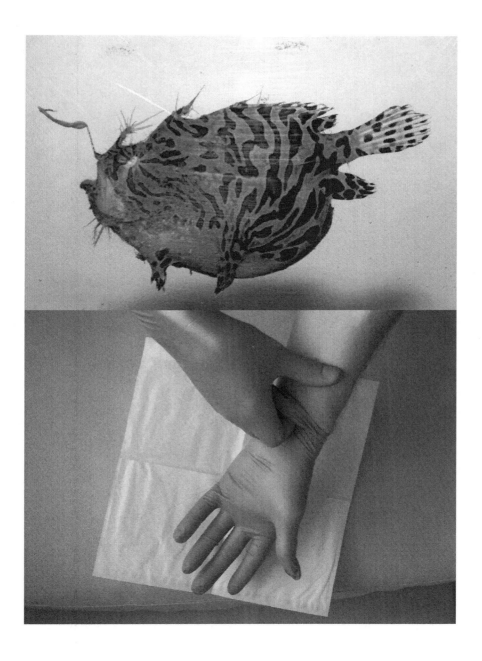

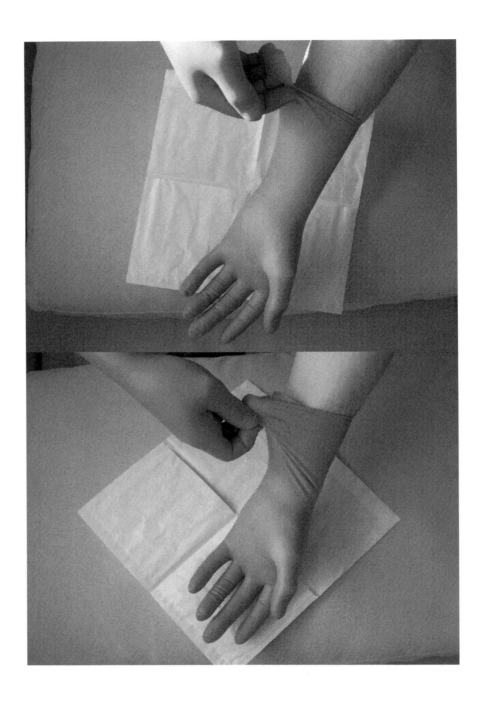

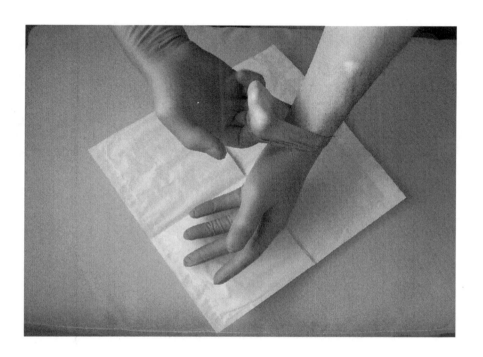

Made in the USA
Monee, IL
25 November 2019

17466549R00028